DATA ANALYTICS

FOR BEGINNERS

Also by Victor Finch

Blockchain Technology: The Essential Quick & Easy Blueprint To Understand Blockchain Technology and Conquer the Next Thriving Economy! Get Your First Mover Advantage Now!

Bitcoin: The Only Complete Quick & Easy Guide To Mastering Bitcoin and Digital Currencies - Make More Money with Bitcoins

Smart Contracts: The Essential Quick & Easy Blueprint To Understand Smart Contracts and Be Ahead of Competition! Get Your Smart Edge Now!

YOUR ULTIMATE GUIDE TO LEARN
AND MASTER DATA ANALYTICS

DATA ANALYTICS

GET YOUR BUSINESS INTELLIGENCE RIGHT

FOR BEGINNERS

ACCELERATE GROWTH AND CLOSE MORE SALES

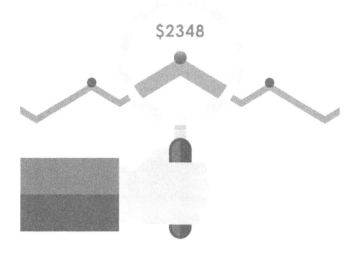

$2348

VICTOR FINCH

AUVA PRESS

Trademarks:

Auva Press and the Auva Press logo are trademarks or registered trademarks and may not be used without written permission. All other trademarks are the property of their respective owners and use in an editorial fashion to the benefit of the trademark owner, with no intention of infringement of the trademark. Auva Press is not associated with any product or vendor mentioned in this book.

FIRST EDITION

ISBN-13: 978-1-5466-4191-9
ISBN-10: 1-5466-4191-2

Editor: Michelle Gabel
Cover Designer: Gina Cassey

To friendship and to my family,
who make my world more meaningful

PREFACE

Companies have had access to available data and, until recently, they were outsourcing data analysts to provide smaller insights into the usefulness of their data. However, today's interest in data analytics is unprecedented. While previous analysis focused only on a few specialized functions, today they focus on all functions, from procurement and marketing to financial. They pay attention to virtually all departments in an organization and the ways in which analytics can improve the performance of these sectors.

But why is that happening only now, you may wonder.

Today, the global economic environment in which companies are operating has changed fast. Companies must not only compete on ROI within the shortest time but also deal with stiff competition from traditional competitors and minimal time to market. In addition to these challenges, these firms have to contend with the demographic changes on one hand and, on the other hand, the new web 2.0 technologies.

VICTOR FINCH

This book was written with the complex and fast-paced volatile markets in mind.

It explores all the basics of data analytics and the role of data analytics in organizations and businesses that can leverage today's data analytics to promote their bottom line.

CONTENTS

Chapter 1

Introduction

Welcome to the world of data scientists! In this chapter, we explore all the concepts about data analysis that should help you get started. By the end of the chapter, you should have a complete picture and possess relevant information regarding data analytics.

Before we get started, let's answer the question: "What is data?"

The word data evokes different meanings depending on the context in which it is used. In measurements or statistics, data is information that forms the basis for reasoning, discussion, or calculations. For instance, facts about the performance of an organization or economic performance of a country represent a type of data.

In computers and computer science, the word data refers to raw facts such as numbers, characters, images, or information captured by any method of recording which forms the basis for assessment and decision-making processes regarding some future actions.

The majority of people believe that data becomes meaningful only when it is interpreted or processed. Whenever we closely examine data to find patterns in it, we are actually using it as a component that generates knowledge.

Understanding data requires an awareness that it can be collected in any form; it could be numbers, pictures, maps, words or even newspaper articles.

I know you are wondering which data format is best.

All the formats are good depending on what you would like to analyze and depends on the types of data. Let's explore the types of data in data analysis.

Types of data

The type of data we can collect can be either qualitative or quantitative.

Qualitative data

Data is qualitative if it can be described with words. Simply said, whatever you observe you can record, such as colors, observations, odor, spatial relationships, or texture.

For instance, suppose you are a marine biologist studying the behavior and activities of dolphins. Surely, you will identify different dolphins within the group and frequently observe them. This can be daily, weekly, monthly or yearly. If you will be recording detailed observations, then the qualitative data might include the following:

- The colors of dolphin range from gray to white.
- When placed in a pod, the dolphins act playfully.
- Dolphins have smooth skins.

Quantitative data

The data that we say is quantitative must have numeric values. Ideally, such data must be objective, meaning that it must be the same regardless who measures it. For instance, in qualitative data, people can observe colors differently and the same dolphin can appear lighter, darker, or might seem to have a different shade.

However, in quantitative data, the collected data must have the same values. For instance, measurements such as length, mass, temperature, time, concentration, and frequency will always be objective. Going back to our earlier example of research on dolphins, the following quantitative data might be collected:

- There are thirteen dolphins in the pod.
- Dolphins eat an equivalent of 10-12% of their body mass each day.
- The sonar frequency that dolphins use is approximately 100 kHz.

Now that you understand what data entails, let's examine the importance of data analytics to businesses.

Importance of data analytics to businesses

Organizations collect process and provide reports—whether on a daily, weekly, monthly or annual basis—

on large volumes of data. It is often said that the average manager in an organization spends at least two hours per day hunting for data to find insights that can help in decision-making.

Half of the information that is collected later turns out to be useless, which means only one thing: companies should find efficient means to turn their data into insightful and usable information. Data analysis in businesses can be enhanced by establishing adequate applications, best practices, skills, and implement necessary technologies that are responsible for investigation and analysis of business performance.

When used properly, data analytics has the ultimate aim of achieving a strategic decision-making and defining the future.

Benefits of data management

Here is why you should consider investing in data management:

#1: It helps in establishing a dialogue with consumers.

It is fact that today's customers are extremely difficult to understand. They shop around from several media channels before purchasing something. They also demand the best treatment, before they become loyal to a particular brand. Data management allows customer profiling and a better understanding of their needs and requirements.

#2: It allows re-examination of products and their improvement

Proper data management can help in understanding the way in which your customers perceive your product or service. Analysis of data, especially the data related to social media, allows you to understand your customers' demands and segment the market based on geographical locations and time zones.

#3: It allows successful risk analysis

The success of your company will not depend only on how well you run your company but a number of other factors, such as social and economic factors, that are vital for the successful promotion of a particular product or service.

Predictive analysis of data, which is hinged on proper data management, will allow data scanning for helpful insights that can help in keeping up with latest developments in a competitive environment. For instance, detailed health-analytics on your suppliers and customers can help in taking appropriate actions to prevent default risks.

#4: Secure data

Map the entire database landscape across all levels of your companies with data management tools. These mappings will provide you with insights to understand threats and vulnerabilities that you are facing. In fact, you can detect sensitive and confidential data that potentially can be exploited by malicious users.

#5: New revenue streams generation

Helpful insights and analysis regarding organization, market processes, and customers that are important for your organization can be obtained with data management tools. Additionally, you can sell the data as non-personalized trends to large firms that are operating in the same market segment. Doing this will expand your revenue base.

#6: Tailor website in real-time to suit the needs of your client

Data management allows you to personalize the content, the look, and the feel of your website in real-time to suit each consumer visiting your website. For instance, you can customize your website based on parameters such as gender, nationality and time zone. For instance, Amazon's use of real-time item-based and collaborative filtering has improved revenue output.

#7: Lower maintenance costs

Traditionally, companies have used various estimation techniques to determine the lifespan of certain equipment based on the depreciation. Consequently, some of these firms have ended up replacing technology after using it for only a few years, although the equipment was still useful.

Data management tools can overcome such impractical and costly estimations for an organization. Application of data management tools will provide a more cost-effective solution and tracking capabilities.

Challenges of data management

Despite massive benefits, utilizing data management poses challenges that hinder the organization from realizing its maximum profit. Data scientists still encounter many problems when it comes to management of data in an organization. If you are dealing with large and unstructured data—that is sometimes called big data—you will not only worry about the ways in which to store the data but also how to ensure its security.

Some challenges that are related to data management include the following:

#1: Exponential data growth

Data experts estimate that data collected in organizations is growing at a rate of 45 percent per year, which is a rampant and exponential growth that companies cannot afford to ignore. The bad thing is that most of the growth is stemming from unstructured and semi-structured data. Management of big data requires disruptive technologies that differ from the current relational systems, which focus on structured data.

#2: Rapid increase of data velocity

Organizations are dealing with fast-changing data that has a short period relevancy. This fact calls for innovative approaches that can help an organization obtain helpful insights.

#3: Data extends across several organizations

In the past, data was strictly centralized but that has changed in our modern and fast-paced times. Data is now being repurposed across several businesses and beyond. The propagation of such data is increased by the need to be used in new applications, services, and repositories.

#4: Data is emerging from new sources

Organizations embrace new systems and create data from new sources that did not exist before. These new sources come with varying needs to access data, protect it, secure it and retain it.

#5: Regulations compliance

Companies must align their data with the changing government regulations. Therefore, companies should know which data to keep, which to dispose, the location of sensitive data, and who has permissions to access that data.

For instance, in healthcare data integration, healthcare providers must be in a position to understand various legislations that regulate the storage, processing, and dissemination of information.

Business intelligence

The current business environment is complex, ever-evolving and unpredictable. These changes—such as consumer needs, globalization, and government regulations—provide both opportunities and challenges for the majority of organizations. It is also not a secret that today's firms are relying on computerized systems to provide business support.

For instance, decision support systems and executive support systems can provide the right information one needs to make sound decisions. The primary function of business intelligence is to help in bridging the gap between an organization's status, which is dictated by the ever-evolving and unpredictable environment, and its desired position.

Ideally, business intelligence provides a framework that supports decision-making processes in an organization. Business intelligence combines data warehousing, predictive business analytics, strategy, performance, and user interface in order to help organizations attain a strategic competitive advantage. Business intelligent applications receive data from the internal and external environment.

Data is captured and stored in a warehouse where it is organized and summarized accordingly. Authorized users can access the data and process it to obtain the desired information, which is shared with executives to make informed strategic decisions.

Smart contracts

Smart contracts are computer program codes with the ability to facilitate, execute, and enforce negotiations or performance of an agreement (contract) using the Blockchain technology. These codes can act as substitutes for legal contracts as contracts are encoded in a computer programming language as a set of instructions.

The potential to link smart contracts to data science is perhaps one of the first steps towards creating a new world of opportunities. With advances in IoT that are connected to cloud computing, wireless sensors, and small computer chips, smart contracts are gaining more popularity.

Data science capabilities joint with smart contracts may promote self-enforcing financial contracts—that execute without a third party. For instance, a farmer can hedge his/her farm produce by using smart contracts, which are dependent on various future prices that are computed, based on prevailing data analytics.

If the conditions for the smart contracts are met, the system can automatically send payments to the farmer. This also applies to all future smart contracts because the farmer will have a physical presence in the available measures readily incorporated into legal systems in cases when the produce is not transferred.

Regardless, smart contracts may immediately find their potentials in digital transfer of goods and services where payment and transfer of payments are automatic. Depending on the type of the contractual agreement, such automation may save billions of dollars and improve the efficiency of operations.

However, the use of smart contracts in these areas is yet to be seen. Enforcement of smart contracts in code form still represents a challenge due to the prevailing laws and regulations that are currently in practice. The current issues have to be resolved in order to realize the true potentials of smart contracts in data science.

Chapter 2

Basics of Data Analytics

For you to become a professional data scientist and find employment in data mining and business intelligence firms, you have to understand the fundamentals of data analytics. The goal of this chapter is to provide all the key concepts of data analytics.

By the end of the chapter, you should be in a position to describe different types of analytics, common terminologies used in analytics, tools and basic prerequisites for analytics as well as the workflow of data analytics.

Types of analytics

Raw data is not different from crude oil. These days, any person or institution with a moderate budget can collect large volumes of raw data. Nevertheless, the collection itself should not be the end goal. Organizations that can extract meanings from the collected raw data are the ones that can compete in today's complex and unpredictable environment.

Although people use the word "analytics" to imply different things, analytics represents the core of any data refinement process. If your sphere of interest is in marketing and you would like to understand data analytics, you should first gain an insight into different types of analytics. Analytics includes the following types:

- Descriptive
- Diagnostic
- Prescriptive
- Exploratory
- Predictive

- Mechanistic
- Casual
- Inferential

#1: Descriptive analytics

The focus of descriptive analytics is to summarize the situation in an organization. Descriptive analytics examines the raw data or content to answer questions such as:

- What happened?
- What is happening?

Conventional business intelligence and visualizations, such as the bar charts, pie charts, line graphs, or generated narratives, characterize descriptive analytics. Descriptive analytics can be used when assessing credit risk in a bank. In such a case, examination of past financial performance of a client can predict his or her financial performance. Descriptive analytics is useful in providing insights into sales cycles such as categorizing customers based on their preferences.

#2: Diagnostic analytics

As the name suggests, diagnostic analytics is used to unearth or to determine why something happened. For example, if you are conducting a social media marketing campaign, you may be interested in assessing the number of likes, reviews, mentions, followers or fans. Diagnostic analytics can help distil thousands of mentions into a single view so that the campaign can be adjusted and be more efficient.

#3: Prescriptive analytics

While most data analytics provides general insights on the subject, prescriptive analytics provides a "laser-like" focus to answer precise questions. For instance, in the healthcare industry, you can use prescriptive analytics to measure the number of patients who are clinically obese.

Prescriptive analytics can allow you to add filters in obesity, such as obesity with diabetes and cholesterol levels, to find out where treatments should focus.

#4: Exploratory analytics

Exploratory analytics is an analytical approach that primarily focuses on identifying general patterns in the raw data to identify outliers and features that might not have been anticipated using other analytical types. To use this approach, you have to understand where the outliers are occurring and how other environmental variables relate to making informed decisions.

For example, in biological data monitoring, several stressors can affect sites and, therefore, stressor correlations represent valuable information in relating stressor variables and biological response variables. The scatterplots and correlation coefficients can provide insightful information on the relationships between the variables.

However, when analyzing different variables, the basic methods of multivariate visualization are necessary to provide greater insights.

#5: Predictive analytics

Predictive analytics implies the use of data, machine-learning techniques, and statistical algorithms to determine the likelihood of results based on historical data. The primary goal of predictive analytics is to help go beyond what has happened and provide the best possible assessment of what is likely to happen in future.

Predictive models use recognizable results to create a model that can predict values for different types of data or create new data. Modeling the results is significant because it provides predictions that represent the likelihood of the target variable—such as revenue—based on the estimated significance from a set of input variables. Classification and regression models are the most popular models used in predictive analytics.

Predictive analytics can be used in banking systems to detect fraud cases, measure the levels of credit risks, and maximize the cross-sell and up-sell opportunities in an organization. This helps in retaining valuable clients.

#6: Mechanistic analytics

As the name suggests, mechanistic analytics allows big data scientists to understand alterations or variables in procedures, which can result in variables change. The results of mechanistic analytics are determined by equations in engineering and physical sciences. In addition, they allow data scientists to determine parameters if they know the equation.

#7: Causal analytics

Causal analytics allows big data scientists to figure out what is likely to happen if one component of the variable is changed. In this approach, a number of random variables determine what is likely to happen even though non-random studies can be used to infer causations. This approach to analytics is appropriate when dealing with large volumes of data.

#8: Inferential analytics

This approach to analytics takes into account different theories related to societies and the world to determine certain aspects of a large population. When you use inferential analytics, you will be required to gather smaller samples of information from the population and use it as a basis to infer information about the larger population.

Common terminologies used in data analytics

As you plan to begin using data analytics to achieve your goals, you must be aware of the common terminology used in data analytics.

- Business Intelligence (BI). It refers to the development of intelligent applications, which are capable of extracting data from both the internal and external environment to help in strategic decision-making.
- Automatic identification and capture (AIDC). It refers to any method can automatically identify and collect data on items and store them in a computer system.
- Avro. This is a data serialization system that facilitates encoding of a database schema in Hadoop.
- Behavioral analytics. It involves data about people's behavior to infer their intent and predict their future actions.
- Big Data Scientist. A professional who can develop algorithms that make sense from big data.
- Cascading. It is used in Hadoop and provides a higher level of abstraction, which allows developers to create complex jobs using different programming languages in the JVM.

- Cassandra. Cassandra is an open source distributed database system developed by Facebook that is designed to deal with large volumes of data.

- Classification analysis. It is a systematic process of obtaining crucial and relevant information about raw data and its metadata.

- Database. It represents a digital collection of logically related and shared data.

- Database administrator (DBA). The term refers to a certified professional who is responsible for developing and maintaining the integrity of the database.

- Database management system (DBMS). This uses software that creates and manipulates database systems in a structured format.

- Data cleansing. The term refers to the process of reviewing and revising data to eliminate duplicate entries, correct spelling mistakes and add missing data.

- Data collection. It entails any process that leads to the acquisition of data.

- Data-directed decision-making. The phrase refers to the database as the basis to support making crucial decisions.

- Data exhaust. The byproduct that is created by a person who uses a database system.

- Data feed. It allows any person to receive a stream of data such as RSS.

- Data governance. It implies a set of processes that promotes the integrity of the data stored in a database system.

- Data integration. The act of combining data from diverse and disparate sources and presenting it in a single coherent and unified view is called data integration.

- Data integrity. Refers to the validity or correctness of data stored in a database. It ensures accuracy, timeliness, and completeness of data.

- Data migration. It is a process of moving data from one storage location or server to another while maintaining its format.

- Data mining. It entails the process of obtaining patterns or knowledge from large sets of databases.

- Data science. This discipline incorporates the use of statistics, data visualization, machine learning, computer programming and data mining database to solve complex problems in organizations.

- Data scientist. The term refers to a professional who is knowledgeable in data science.

- Machine learning. Using algorithms to allow computers to analyze data for extracting information to take specific actions based on specific events or patterns.

- MongoDB. A NoSQL database system is oriented to documents and developed under the open source concept. It uses JSON to save data structures in documents with a dynamic scheme.

- Qualitative analysis. This term refers to a process of analyzing qualitative data by interpreting words and texts.

- Quantitative analysis. It implies a process of analyzing quantitative data by interpreting numerical data.

- Quartiles. The lower (Q1) quartile is the value below for which the bottom 25% of any sampled data lies, and the upper (Q3) quartile is the value above which the upper 25% of sampled data lies.

- R. It is an open source programming language for performing data analysis.

- Random sample. Every member of a given population has an equal chance of being selected in a random sample. The random sample is the representative of the population that is being studied.

- Representative. This refers to the extent to which the sampled data reflects accurately the characteristics of the selected population in an experiment.

- Research process. The process researchers or data scientists employ to answer research questions and hypotheses.

- Research question. It refers to a specific question that guides the research process.

- Sample. A subset (n) that is selected from the entire population (N).

- Standard deviation. It is a descriptive statistic—which is a measure of dispersion, or spread—of sampled data around the mean.

- The standard error of the mean. It is a measure of the accuracy of the sampled mean as an estimate of the entire population mean.

- Hypothesis. A precise statement, which is a proposition, that relates to the research question that is to be tested.

- Independent variable. It refers to the variable that determines the values of the other dependent (response) variable. For instance, it can show the changes in blood pressure and its relation to aging.

Tools and basic prerequisites for a beginner in data analytics

By now, you might be wondering where to start to become a professional data analyst.

To become a professional data scientist, here is what you should learn:

- Mathematics
- Excel
- Basic SQL
- Web development

Let's see the roles of these fields in data analytics.

#1: Mathematics

Data analytics is all about numbers. If you relish working with numbers and algebraic functions, then you will love data analytics. However, if you do not like numbers, you should begin to cultivate a positive attitude. Also, be willing to learn. The truth is that the world of data analytics is fast-paced and unpredictable. Therefore, you cannot be contented. You should be ready to learn new technologies that are springing up to deal with changes in data management.

#2: Excel

Excel is the most all-around and common business application for data analytics. While many data scientists graduate with functional specific skill—such as data mining, visualization, and statistical applications—almost all these skills can be learned and applied in Excel. Learning the basic concepts of Excel, such as workbooks, worksheets, the formula bar and the ribbon represent a great first step.

Once you are familiar with concepts of Excel, you can proceed to learn the basic formulas such as sum, average, if, count, lookup, date, max and min, get pivot data. As you become more comfortable with basic formulas, try out the complex formulas for regression and chi-square distributions.

#3: Basic SQL

Excel provides tools to slice and dice data. However, it assumes the data is already stored in your computer system. What about data collection and storage? As you will learn about seasoned data scientists, the best approach to deal with data is getting it or pulling it directly from its source. Excel does not provide you with these functionalities.

Relational database management systems (RDBMS) such as SQL Server, MS Access, and MySQL, provide support for data collection procedures. To master relational database management systems, you should be good in SQL (Structured Query Language), which is the language that underpins all the RDBMS.

To fast track the mastery of SQL, you should understand how the following statements/commands are used:

- Select

- From
- Where
- Group By
- Having
- Order By

Besides mastering the basic SQL commands, you should also understand the reason behind the use of primary keys, foreign keys, and candidate keys in this DBMS.

#4: Basic web development

I know you are thinking that web development is an oddball with regard to data analytics. However, mastery of web development will be an added bonus to your data scientist career. If you want to work for consumer internet companies or work for IoT companies such as IBM, AWS, and Microsoft Azure, you have to be good in internet programming tools such as HTML, JavaScript, and PHP.

Advanced tools and prerequisites for data analytics

If you wish to take your professional career to the next level, then basic prerequisites for data analytics may be insufficient. Here are other advanced tools and requirements:

#1: Hadoop

Hadoop is a cloud-computing platform that can perform highly parallelized operations on big data. An open-source software framework stores big data and allows applications to run on it in form of clusters. One advantage of Hadoop is that at allows users to store and process massive storage of data of any type. Because of enormous processing power, Hadoop is suited for analysis of big data with virtually limitless simultaneous tasks.

#2: R programming

Every person that starts the journey of data science usually faces the common problem of selecting the best programming language. Today, there are a couple of programming languages that can perform data analytics. Each of these programming languages has its own fair share of pros and cons. However, R is very useful for data analytics, especially in the field of statistics, due to its versatile nature. It is an open source software that provides data scientists a variety of features for analyzing data.

R is popular in data analytics because:

- It is simple, well developed and a programming language that supports loops, recursive functions, conditionals, and input/output facilities.
- It provides operators that can perform calculations on vectors, arrays, matrices and lists.
- It has storage possibilities, therefore, data analysts can effectively handle their data.
- It has graphical possibilities that data analysts can use to display processed data.

#3: Python programming

Python is a very powerful, open source, and flexible programming language that is easy to learn, use, and has powerful libraries for data manipulation, management, and analysis. It is simple and resembles MatLab, C or C++, or Java. If you have basic knowledge in any of these programming languages, you will not have a problem with Python.

In addition, Python combines features of general-purpose programming language and those of analytical and quantitative computing. In the recent past, Python found its application in scientific computing in quantitative domains, in finance, physics, oil, gas and signal processing.

Similarly, Python has been used to develop popular scalable web applications such as YouTube. Because of its popularity, Python can help in big data and business analytics in science, engineering and other areas of scalable computing. You can use Python's inbuilt libraries such as Panda and NumPy to help in data analytics as it also integrates well with existing independent IT infrastructure systems. Among modern programming languages, the productivity of Python-based applications is legendary.

#4: Database proficiency tools

Database proficiency tools—such as SQL Server, MS Access, MongoDB, and MySQL—support procedures for data collection, storage, and processing. To master these systems, you should be good in SQL (Structured Query Language), the language that underpins all these systems.

To fast track the mastery of SQL, you should understand how the following statements/commands are used:

- Select
- From
- Where
- Group By
- Having
- Order By

Besides mastering the basic SQL commands, you should also understand the reason behind the use of primary keys, foreign keys, and candidate keys in these systems.

#5: MatLab

MatLab is a very powerful, flexible and open source programming language that is easy to learn, use and has powerful libraries for data manipulation, management, and analysis. Its simple syntax is easy to learn and resembles C or C++. If you have basic skills in these programming languages, you will not have a problem with MatLab.

In addition, MatLab combines the features of general-purpose programming language and those of analytical and quantitative computing. In the recent past, MatLab has been applied in scientific computing and quantitative domains.

Similarly, MatLab has been used to develop popular scalable web applications such as YouTube. Just as Python, MatLab can help you with big data and business analytics in science, engineering and other areas of scalable computing, because it also integrates well with existing independent IT infrastructure systems.

#6: Perl

Perl is a dynamic and high-level programming language that has application in data analytics. Larry Wall originally developed it as a scripting language for UNIX, Perl has the flexibility to develop robust and scalable systems.

With the advent of the internet in 1990's, Perl usage exploded. Besides providing dominant features of CGI programming, Perl has also become a key language for data analysis because of its rich set of analysis libraries.

Java and its Java-based frameworks are deeply rooted in the skeletons of virtually all the biggest Silicon Valley tech companies. When you look at Twitter, LinkedIn, or Facebook, you will find that Java is the backbone programming language for all the data engineering infrastructures. Unlike Python and R, Java does not provide the same features of data analytics. However, when it comes to excellent performance on a large scale, it is unparalleled.

Java's speed makes it one of the best languages for developing large-scale systems. While Python is significantly faster than R but compared to Python, Java provides an even greater performance. For this reason, Twitter, Facebook, and LinkedIn have picked Java as the backbone of their systems. However, Java may not be appropriate for statistical modeling.

Today, the vast majority of data analytics use R, Java, MatLab, and Python for data analysis. Nevertheless, there is still some gap since there is no language that is one-stop-shop for data analysis needs. Julia is a new programming language that can fill the gaps with respect to improving visualizations and libraries for data analysis.

Even though the Julia programming community is in infancy, more and more programmers will soon realize its potentials in data analysis and adopt it.

Data analytics workflow

Data analytics workflow can be explained in the following steps:

- Preparation phase
- Analysis phase
- Reflection phase
- Dissemination phase

Let's dive in to explore these phases.

#1: Preparation stage

Before you analyze your data, you must acquire the data and reformat it into in a manner that is suitable for computation. You can acquire data from the following sources:

- Data files from online repositories such as public websites, for instance, the U.S. Census data sets.

- Data files streamed on-demand through APIs, such as for instance, the Bloomberg financial data stream.
- Physical apparatus such as scientific lab equipment that is connected to computers.
- Data from computer software such as log files from web servers.
- Manual data entry in the spreadsheet files.

#2: Analysis phase

The analysis is at the core of any data analytics activity, which involves writing computer programs or scripts that analyze data to derive helpful insights from it. You can use programming languages such as Python, Perl, MatLab, R, or Hadoop.

#3: Reflection phase

At this stage, you will frequently be alternating between the analysis and the reflection stages as you work on data to obtain the necessary information. While the analysis phase is a purely programming process, the reflection phase requires critical thinking and communication with clients about the obtained outputs.

After inspecting the collected sets of output files, you can take notes if you are dealing with an experiment that is in either physical or digital format.

#4: Dissemination phase

Dissemination is the final phase of data analysis workflow. You can present your results using written reports such as the internal memos, PowerPoint presentations, or business whitepapers. If you are in the academic field, you can publish the academic paper.

Statistical process

The process of data analysis begins with identifying the population from which you will obtain data. Because it is practically impossible to get data on every subject in the population, you should use an appropriate sampling technique to get a sample size that is representative. The statistical process is a four-step phase activity that includes the following:

- Estimate the expected proportion of the population that you want to study. The proportion of that population must be of interest to the study. Previously published literature reviews or studies can serve as the basis for the expected proportion. If in doubt, consult experts in that field to get the correct estimate.

- Determine the confidence interval for use in your analysis. Think of confidence level as the "margin of error" in your sample size. Now, all the empirical estimates are based on a sample that has a certain degree of uncertainty. It is necessary to specify the desired total spectrum of the confidence interval.

- Set the value of the confidence level. This provides the precision or level of uncertainty in the analysis. Typically, a 95% confidence level is widely used. However, a narrow confidence interval that has a high confidence level, such as 99%, is likely to be representative.

- Use the statistical table to estimate your sample size. If the number that is required is too large, you can recalculate it with lower confidence levels or use wider intervals to choose a smaller sample size.

Descriptive and Inferential statistics

Statistics is broadly divided into two fields: descriptive and inferential. Descriptive statistics provides information about the distribution, variations, and the shape of the data. Descriptive statistics analyzes a big chunk of data to provide summary charts, bar graphs, pie charts, using descriptive measures such as:

- Measures of central tendency such as mean, mode, and median.
- Measures of dispersion such as range, variance, and standard deviation.
- Measures of a shape such as skewness.

However, descriptive statistics does not draw conclusions about the population from where the sample was obtained. If you are interested in knowing the relationships and differences within your data, or whether statistical significance exists, you have to use inferential statistics.

Inferential statistics provides these determinations and allows you to generalize your results obtained from the sample size to the larger population. Some of the models you are likely to use for inferential statistics include:

- Chi-square distributions
- Correlation and regression models
- ANOVA
- ANCOVA

Chapter 3

Data Analysis

Data Analysis is the activity of systematically applying both statistical and logical techniques to describe/illustrate, condense/recap, and evaluates raw data. In this chapter, we explore data analysis methods that can help you analyze data.

Below are examples of data analysis methods that you can use for your data:

#1: Decision Tree Analysis

Decision Trees are excellent data analysis tools that can help in choosing an action from several alternatives. Decision trees provide a highly efficient structure that allows examination of options and possible outcomes when opting for either of the available options. In fact, they provide you with a balanced picture of all the risks and rewards that are associated with each possible decision made.

When evaluating various decisions in the decision node, you should note down the cost of each option on the decision line. Thereafter, subtract the total cost from the outcome value to give you a value that denotes the benefit of the decision you are making. Of course, it is always advisable to select the option with the highest benefit.

#2: Regression Analysis

Regression analysis establishes relationships between two or more variables. This technique is appropriate for forecasting purposes, time series modeling and determining the causal effect relationships between two or more variables. For instance, regression analysis model can help in establishing relationships between high speed and reckless driving, and a number of road accidents.

Regression analysis has the following advantages:

- It provides significant relationships between the dependent variable and the independent variable.
- It provides the strength of impacts of multiple independent variables on the dependent variable.

Regression analysis allows comparison of the variables impacts that are measured on different scales. For instance, you may want to establish the effect of price changes and the number of advertising activities in your firm. Such information can help marketing researchers and data scientists to eliminate and evaluate best sets of variables for optimum performance of the organization.

#3: Machine Learning

This is a method of data analysis that automates the process of data analysis by building an analytical model in computers. The model is developed using computer algorithms that iteratively learn from raw data.

Machine learning allows computers to find unknown insights from data without programming computers to look for that data.

The machine was born from pattern recognition in Artificial Intelligence and theory of computation and the belief that computers can "learn" without necessarily requiring programming. The iterative process of machine learning is important in today's big data that is massive and computers help in uncovering hidden insights.

These are the few successful examples of machine learning in action:

- The hyped, driverless Google car
- Online recommendation offers from e-commerce sites such as Amazon and eBay.
- Fraud detection systems.

#4: Social Network Analysis

Social Network Analysis (SNA) is the process through which networks and graph theories investigate social structures such as social media networks, internet memes, collaboration graphs, disease transmissions, and sexual relationships. A social network analysis begins investigating these social structures by examining their nodes—which can be individual actors, peoples, or things in the group—and the edges or the relationships between them.

This method of data analysis has its roots in the scholarly works of early sociologists who underpinned the significance of studying patterns of relations/interactions that connect actors of any given group. Graph theory identifies the "important" actors in the social chain and stands at the core of this method.

The method uses the principle of centrality and prestige to quantify graph theoretic ideas about any individual actor's prominence in the group. By providing summaries for each structural relation, SNA describes structural relationships between group nodes. The group level indices can also be used to provide levels of dispersion or any inequality among the actors.

If you are working on data that requires extensive mining, data aggregation, network propagation modeling, modeling, the behavioral analysis in a group, or location-based interaction analysis, then SNA is the right method to exploit.

#5: Association Rule Analysis

As the name suggests, Association Rule Analysis (ARA)—sometimes called Market Based Analysis (MBA)—is a popular data mining method that determines relative strengths of relationships among a set of items. Support and confidence of the association rule determine the strength of the relationship. For instance, the support for
the rule $A \Rightarrow B$ can be perceived as the probability that the two item sets will occur together. The support of the rule $A \Rightarrow B$ can be simplified mathematically as follows:

$$\frac{transactions\ that\ contain\ every\ item\ in\ A\ and\ B}{all\ transactions}$$

From the above equation, you can note that support is always symmetric. In other words, the support for the rule $A \Rightarrow B$ is the same as the support for rule $B \Rightarrow A$.

Now, the confidence of the association rule $A \Rightarrow B$ can be viewed as a conditional probability. This can be aptly be viewed as the conditional probability of a transaction that contains set B given that it contains the item in set A. Mathematically, this can be simplified as:

$$\frac{transactions\ that\ contain\ every\ item\ in\ A\ and\ B}{transactions\ that\ contain\ the\ items\ in\ A}$$

Association rules are mostly used in markets to predict strengths of relationships among items using predetermined rules. However, they can also be used in other application domains such as the bioinformatics, web mining, medical diagnosis, and scientific data analysis.

#6: Sentiment Analysis

The rapid growth of social media such as Twitter, Facebook and LinkedIn, and blogs, has powered interest in sentiment analysis. With the explosion of reviews, ratings, likes, mentions, recommendations, and other forms of online expression, online opinion plays an extremely significant role for organizations that market their products, identify new opportunities for growth, and maintain their reputation.

Sentiment Analysis (SA) can help organizations filter out the relevant content from "digital noise." So, how does Sentiment Analysis differ from the conventional methods of data analysis?

SA uses natural language processing features, textual analysis, computational linguistics, and biometrics to systematically detect, mine, quantify, and study the affective states and the subjective information. Sentiment analysis is widely used in the analysis of customer's voice by reviewing their survey responses, social media platforms, and healthcare data.

Three approaches are used in sentiment analysis. These are:

- Knowledge-based techniques
- Statistical methods
- Hybrid methods

While knowledge-based techniques classify the text in context and separate it into categories based on unambiguous words—such as happy, afraid, or bored—

statistical methods rely on machine-learning elements such as the latent semantics of the words. For instance, a statement such as "bag of words" can be analyzed using statistical methods by identifying its semantic orientation as opposed to classification based on unambiguous words.

Hybrid methods incorporate both features of knowledge-based and statistical techniques to provide the right mix of elements for sentiment analysis.

#7: Generic Algorithms

A genetic algorithm (GA) is a search heuristic code that resembles the process of natural evolution and generates useful insights in order to optimize search problems. GA systems are used aptly in DNA genome sequencing. While GA systems were created for data mining in DNA sequencing, they are also used for classification-based predictive scenarios for user-defined goals.

For example, the GA system can be used in banking to predict customers' ability to get advanced loans. In this case, the GA can determine whether a customer's credit rating is "good" or "bad" based on parameters such as age, current savings, and income.

Typically, the GA systems perform data mining and check the existing data sets. Those rules that are close to the selected data are picked and mutated. The process is repeated several times until a rule that approaches 100% similarity is reached.

#8: Cluster Analysis

Cluster Analysis—also called segmentation analysis or taxonomy analysis—is an explorative analysis that identifies structures within raw data that should be analyzed. When using cluster analysis, homogeneous groups of subjects that require analysis are selected based on observations, participants, or respondents.

- The process begins by determining groups of subjects that are unknown. Since the process is exploratory in nature, key distinctions between independent and dependent variables should be made.

Chapter 4

Data Mining

The bottom line of data mining is to unearth the "hidden" value in a database. In this chapter, we explore all the basics of data mining, including what it is, its techniques, best practices and mistakes that should be avoided while mining data.

What is data mining?

Data mining is a process of extracting hidden predictive information from large sets of databases. It is a powerful and revolutionary technology that has a great potential in helping companies achieves their strategic competitive advantages.

Data mining tools can help predict future trends and behaviors from large sets of databases. Data mining allows making proactive and knowledge-based driven decisions that promote achieving the desired end goals.

The majority of companies are already collecting and refining massive amounts of readily available data. If you have an existing IT infrastructure such as software and hardware platforms, there is no justifiable reason to invest in data mining because mining tools can easily integrate with new products and systems in your organization.

When implemented on a high-performance system such as client/server and parallel processing computers, data mining can analyze large volumes of data and provide helpful insights in understanding your customers.

How does data mining work?

Data mining depends on modeling to obtain insightful information from large sets of data. Modeling implies building a set of artifacts in a scenario where the answer is already known and serves as a basis for different scenarios.

For instance, if one were searching for a gold ring on Maldives, the first thing to do is to research how many times other people have found a gold ring on Maldives. The information might provide data on people and locations where a ring was found.

Once this information or patterns are noted, they are used to build a model that should help in locating the treasure. Hopefully, a good model built on the available information will help in finding the treasure. That is how data mining works. Every mining process will have its constructed model. If you plan to become a data scientist, your work will provide models based on large databases.

Data mining techniques

Data mining techniques can be classified as follows:

- Association techniques
- Classification techniques

- Clustering techniques
- Decision trees
- Regression techniques

Let's jump in to find out how these techniques are used in data mining.

#1: Association technique

The association technique is a well-known data mining technique. This technique discovers a pattern based on the data regarding relationships between data items in the same transaction. Association rules are mostly used in markets to predict strengths of relationships among items using predetermined rules.

For instance, you may want to determine a customer buying behavior based on historical sales data. However, the association technique can also be used in other application domains such as bioinformatics, web mining, medical diagnosis, and scientific data analysis.

#2: Classification technique

The classification technique is based on machine learning. Machine learning automates the process of data analysis by building an analytical model in computers. The model is developed using computer algorithms that iteratively learn from the raw data. Machine learning allows computers to find data without programming the computer to look for that data.

The classification is used to group each data item into predefined sets of classes or groups. This approach can use mathematical techniques such decision trees, neural networks, statistics and linear programming. For instance, software can be created to learn how to group data items.

#3: Clustering technique

Cluster Analysis is an explorative analysis that identifies structures within raw data that should be analyzed. When using cluster analysis, homogeneous groups of subjects that require analysis based on observations, participants, or respondents should be identified.

The process begins by determining previously unknown groups of subjects. Since the process is exploratory in nature, make key distinctions between independent and dependent variables.

#4: Regression technique

Regression analysis establishes relationships between two or more variables. This technique is appropriate for forecasting purposes, time series modeling, and determining causal effects and relationships between two or more variables. For instance, regression analysis model can help in establishing relationships between high speed and reckless driving and number of road accidents.

Regression analysis allows comparison and impacts of variables that have been measured on different scales. For instance, you may want to establish the relation between price changes and the number of advertising activities in your firm. Such information can help marketing researchers and data scientists to eliminate and evaluate best sets of variables for optimum performance of the organization.

#5: Decision Trees

Decision Trees can help in choosing an action from several given alternatives. They provide a highly efficient structure that allows examination of possible outcomes when selecting any of the available options. In fact, they provide a balanced picture of all the risks and rewards that are associated with each possible decision.

When evaluating various decisions in the decision node, you should note down the cost of each option on the decision line. Thereafter, subtract the total cost from the outcome value to get a value that denotes the benefit of the decision you are making. Naturally, it is always advisable to select the option that gives the highest benefit.

Data Mining Best Practices

Below are best practices for data mining:

- Understand the reasons for data mining. If senior management wants data mining to unearth mundane information, such as figures related to monthly sales, it may not be necessary to spend time on expensive and time-consuming data mining. However, if the senior management wants to determine when a customer ordered specific items on different channels, then data mining may make sense.

- Define goals and strategic objectives your management requires. Which goals do you want to achieve with data mining? Which questions need answers? Answering questions will help to define goals that meet the business objectives.

- Establish if you have the required raw data to use in data mining. For instance, just having information about products, orders, and the customers may not be enough to justify investments in data mining. You need to have detailed customer profiles, order histories, and full website analytic data.

- Identify all the possible data sources. The raw data may originate from many sources, from online analytics, e-commerce databases, social media platforms, and customer support logs, or brick and mortar POS. Knowing the data sources will help in creating better strategies for integration purposes during data mining.

- Determine various data warehouse solutions that will promote the firm's objectives. This is important because each solution and architecture have their own features and restrictions. Understanding their potentials will allow using the tools to your advantage.

- Always define the level of security for your data. Data security and security requirements should be in place to get access to the data that is vital for every organization. Will data require encryption? Will it require a firewall or a backup system?

- Always implement the mining process in phases. Implementing the entire solution can take a longer time making you lose focus. Ensure that you prioritize your data mining needs and complete the process in stages.

- Always understand your data management strategy. When your company's use of data grows and changes, you may realize unusability of some data. Constantly cleaning and confirming is much easier than a massive cleanup exercise. To avoid so many changes in your data, always monitor the database needs.

- Allocate the proper resources. Dealing with a data warehouse demands at least one full-time position. Activities such as maintenance, reporting, and validation are always ongoing. Having a full-time data manager makes sense.

Chapter 5

Data Collection

Excel is very popular and can help you collect, organize and manipulate data in tables. However, typing the data into a spreadsheet and moving the cursor after every entry can be daunting.

Fortunately, Excel provides data entry forms that can ease the pain. With only a sprint of setup and the knowledge where to find forms, Excel allows data collection in a more efficient and simplified manner.

Data Preparation

Setting up the Excel table

Organizing the Excel data table can save a great deal of time and problem solving later. An Excel table is organized in rows and columns. Below is a description of these features:

- **Rows:** Each row represents one chunk of data. In database terminologies, this forms one record. Depending on the nature of the Excel table, a record can be the customer's contact information or an invoice data.

- **Columns:** Each column should only hold one type of data for each record. In database terminologies, this forms one field. If the Excel table holds data about customers, then one field may be the customer name, another one may be the address and so on.

- **Row Headers:** The first row of the Excel table is usually reserved for the column headers. At the row headers, you will place field names such as "Customer Name" and "Customer Address". Excel uses these names as labels for data entry form.

Tips for effective Excel data structure

When creating an Excel data structure, adhere to the following tips:

- All the data should be entered in a single spreadsheet file.
- Always enter variable names in the first row of the spreadsheet file.
- The variable names should not be longer than 8 characters and should start with a letter.
- The variable names should not contain spaces. However, they can start with an underscore character.
- There should be no other text rows such as the titles in the spreadsheet.
- There should be no blank rows appearing in the Excel data.
- If you have multiple groups of data, place them in the same spreadsheet together with variable names that show group membership.
- Avoid using alphabetic characters for values.
- If your data group has two levels, such as Male or Female, code them using 0 and 1 as it allows easier analysis.

67

- For missing data values, always leave cells blank.
- It is a good practice to enter dates using slashes (such as 5/05/2017) and times using colons (such as 12:15 AM).

Now proceed to set up an Excel form, as it should ease your pain.

Setting up the Excel Form

With your Excel data now organized in table structure, highlight the entire data and click on the Home ribbon. While on the Home ribbon, choose Table, and select one of the table styles according to your preference. Proceed as follows:

Now you are ready to create a form. Ensure you have the Forms Button on display. If you are using Excel 2007, the Forms Button will not be available. To display it, use the Quick Access Menu to add it or follow the next steps:

- Right-click any empty space on the Excel ribbon and select "*Customize the Ribbon*".

- In the dialog box that shows up, set "Choose commands from:" to choose Commands that are not in the Ribbon.
- On the right-hand side of the Excel Window, select Data and click on the "*New Group*" button.
- On the left-hand side of the Window, click "Form…"
- Finally, with both the "Form…" and New Group (Custom) highlighted, click the Add >> button.

Now you can set up your form.

The headers specified in the top row of the Excel table will now become field names. By default, the dialog box that crops when you start the Form Wizard shows the first existing record that you entered in the table. You can browse and change the existing records with the "Find Next" and "Find Prep" buttons.

To add a new record or row to the Excel table, simply click the "New" button. When you finish, click the "Close" button. This way, you will find the process of data entry using Excel much simpler than you have thought.

Cleaning Data

Cleaning up data is one of the final phases of formatting data and preparing it for analysis. For the majority of data analysts, cleaning data is a thankless, dull, laborious, and painstaking job. However, cleaning data is crucial for the success of data analysis. What is data cleaning and why is it important?

As the name suggests, cleaning data is the process of removing elements in data that are irrelevant such as duplicate entries or extraneous characters. The primary goal of data cleaning is to ensure the data is error-free.

How can you clean up your data?

The first step towards cleaning up Excel data is copying the data from the original data sheet to a new sheet, which you can call an interim data sheet. Before you begin cleaning, you should assign each row in Excel an ID number. This way, if you delete a row, seemingly because it is a duplicate, you can easily note from the gaps in ID numbers which rows were deleted.

With this done, you can now start cleaning data.

- To manage the duplicate records, use the formula CONCATENATE () to help merge duplicated records.
- To strip out undesirable characters from data, use the Find/Replace command to help locate all the undesired characters and their replacements.
- To locate out-of-range values, use the formula LEN () in order to determine conditional formatting and the length of the strings used.
- To remove extra spaces, use the formula TRIM ().
- To capitalize the first letter of each string, use the formula PROPER ()
- To remove all the non-printable characters from text, use the formula CLEAN ().
- To convert text to number, use the function VALUE ().
- To convert numbers or text to a new text format, use the function TEXT ().

Referencing Data

After the data has been cleared, the next stage involves processing it. However, before processing, the way in which data in the cells is accessed can have an impact on the results. Cell referencing is the process where cells, or a range of cells in the worksheet, are used in a formula so Excel can find values of the data that a formula will compute.

For a majority of Excel formulas, you can use cell references to refer to:

- Data from one or more continuous cells on the Excel sheet.
- Data that is contained in different areas of the Excel sheet.
- Data located in other Excel sheets but only within the same workbook.

Excel has two types of referencing: absolute and relative.

By default, all the cell references in Excel will have relative references. Relative means that when the data is copied across multiple cells, it will change its values based on the relative position of the rows and columns. For instance, if the formula =A2+B2 is copied from row 2 to row 3, the new formula becomes =A3+B3. This referencing style is convenient when you need to repeat the same calculation across several rows and columns.

Unlike relative references, absolute references do not change when the formulas are copied or changed. You can use absolute references to keep values of a row or a column constant.

An absolute reference is specified in a formula by adding the dollar sign ($). The dollar sign can precede the column reference, the row reference, or even both.

Aggregating Data

The Excel Power Query—an add-in that is used for data discovery, reshaping and combining data emanating from different sources—is one of the powerful elements of Excel that can aggregate data. With the Power Query, you can transform data into any format that is ready for use in the pivot tables, reports, and so much more.

The Power Query can allow you to:

- Add your data sources such as the Excel tables, the CSV files, database tables, and web pages.

- Press the buttons in the Power Query window so you transform the data.
- Output the data to your worksheet or any data model that is ready for pivot tables.

The Power Query can be downloaded from the official Microsoft website. Depending on the nature of your OS—whether it is a 32-bit or 64-bit—select and install the right version. Once it has been installed, you will see the Power Query Editor in Excel ribbon next time you launch Excel.

With the Power Query, you can aggregate columns of any linked table. For instance, you can aggregate the sum of the order details for each order. The Power Query Editor will provide all the commands needed to aggregate the table. Once you select the column header that contains the related table link, simply click on Aggregate and select the appropriate aggregate functions.

Visualizing Data

Excel provides an excellent range of tools that can help visualize data. You can exploit the full range of these analytical and visualization tools to explore your data and create color-coded data values reports and interactive slides. The following guidelines should be considered when visualizing data in Excel:

- Always use the Power View when exploring data with a range of data visualizations. If you are working with PowerPivot data model, the Power View is particularly significant when you want to establish relationships between data that are in multiple tables.

- You can use the Power Map to show changes in geographically related dispersed data values over time.

- Use the native Pivot Charts and the conditional formatting when creating data visualizations in workbooks that will be launched in versions of Excel that do not support Power View or the Power Map.

Below are common tools that you can use to visualize the data:

#1: Pie charts

If you want to visualize data in form of slices, consider using pie charts. Pie charts usually display the contribution of each value—or the slice—to a total (pie). Pie charts rely on one data series. Below is an example of a pie chart:

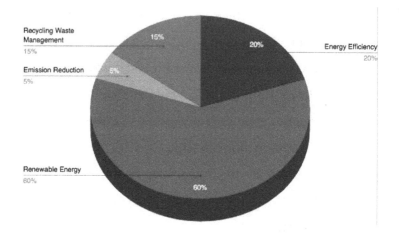

#2: Bar Graphs

Bar graphs can be used to display data in a form of horizontal or vertical rectangular bars. The bars levels to an appropriate level to define values on the plane. Below is an example of a bar chart:

Decrease in Body Fat Percentage by Diet

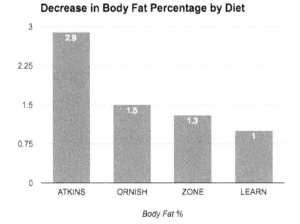

Body Fat %

#3: Line Graphs

Line graphs are used to compare changes that take place over a period of time for more than one group of data. Below is an example of a line graph:

#4: Histogram

A histogram—often called the frequency polygon—is a graph formed by joining the midpoints of histogram column tops. Histograms are used when depicting data from continuous variables. One common misconception is that histogram is based on height which is wrong. Histogram is based on area to indicate the frequency of occurrences for each range.

Below is an example of a histogram:

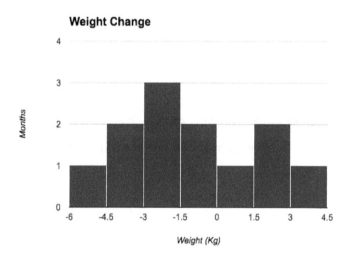

Now, you may wonder how do you differentiate a histogram and a bar graph? If you take a look at the bar graph earlier, you will notice the differences between the histogram and bar graph.

1. The horizontal axis is in ranges in histogram and categories in bar graph

2. There are no gaps in histogram but gaps are visible in bar graph.

#5: Scatter Plots

The scatter plots are similar to the line graphs because they also use the horizontal and vertical axes to plot data points. However, scatterplots have a very specific purpose—to show how one variable is affected or is related to another. Below is an example of a scatter plot:

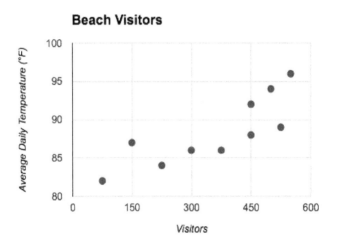

Chapter 6

Data Analytics Patterns

If you know how best to frame the right questions related to the raw data that will be analyzed, you may end up finding patterns that you did not expect. That is the beauty of data mining. It allows uncovering hidden insightful patterns that may not be discovered using conventional methods.

How to Recognize Patterns

When summarizing the characteristics of all the spatial distributions, previously hidden patterns may become evident. But what can the patterns tell you?

Understanding properties of data distribution is critical in understanding appropriate analytical methods and coming to reasonable conclusions. Spatial patterns deal with both distributions of data, or attributes, and spatial arrangements of locations. Summarizing spatial characteristics infers the patterns in your data.

Continuous surfaces that display the intensity of features, or data values, based on sample observations, can show areas of concentrations. When associating one type of event with another—such as the control group—interesting differences can be detected in data.

Spatial clustering of data can be an indicator of patterns of underlying processes that are similar. Areas of local concentrations with high or low values within large datasets can be identified and patterns can become obvious.

Types of patterns

Patterns can be grouped into following categories:
82

- Approximate pattern. These are patterns or trends that are inferred from a noisy data, which, in most cases, is found in disparate locations.

- Statistical pattern. It is a pattern that comes from statistical formula application to a set of data.

- Regression pattern. It is a pattern that arises from correlations between two or more variables.

Chapter 7

Business Intelligence Concepts and Applications

Business intelligence combines data warehousing, predictive business analytics, strategy, performance, and user interface to help organizations attain a strategic competitive advantage. Business intelligent applications receive data from an internal and external environment. Data is captured and stored in a warehouse where it is organized and summarized according to its utilization. BI concepts can be applied in the following industries:

#1: Banking

BI systems are used in banks to predict customers' ability to take advanced loans. In this case, BI determines whether a customer's credit rating is "good" or "bad" based on parameters such as age, current savings, and income.

#2: Retail

BI provides retail firms of all sizes with ways not only to improve their operational efficiencies and cost-effectiveness but also mechanisms in order to achieve differentiation strategies.

#3: Logistics

When applied in supply chain and management, BI scales up internal efficiencies to allow organizations use their operational data for trend analysis and constructing better business strategies to achieve profitability.

#4: Manufacturing

BI can be used for gathering, organizing, and processing information from all levels of a company. The BI software can sift through large sets of data across the supply chain and provide insightful information to the company for better decisions making with regard to inventories.

#5: Public Sector

In addition to providing classical merits such as customer segmentation, propensity to buy, customer profitability, and similar, BI can also help governments design fraud detection systems and personnel attrition.

#6: Medical and Healthcare

BI is a must for healthcare providers to standardize data, reduce healthcare data redundancy and costs while complying with industry standards for enhanced efficiencies.

#7: Customer Relationship Management

BI platforms can consolidate data Into a central place and allow organizations to improve and expand their existing relationships while enhancing customer service by using historical data related to all the previous customer interactions.

#8: Insurance

BI platforms, through data gathering, extracting relevant information, and transforming it into actionable reports for improved profitability, can provide insurance investment managers with transparency and visibility they require for their investment portfolios.

Chapter 8

Case Studies

Below are case studies for organizations that have adopted BI as part of their competitive strategies:

Case Study #1: Columbia State Bank

The Columbia State Bank deployed BI for Precision from Fiserv effectively to manage its high volume of data that was problematic when using conventional technologies. The bank needed to standardize the development and distribution of its reports in a seamless manner. Cumbersome third-party software and duplicate reports caused inefficiencies.

After a thorough evaluation of their operations, the Bank decided to use Business Analytics for Precision to gain efficiency and control over its financial reporting processes. As part of the larger enterprise-wide process management ingenuity, the bank opted for BI for Precision to transform the process of reporting.

Report development, dissemination and research became more flexible while at the same time saved money.

The Business Analytics system has had a major impact on Columbia State Bank's organizational efficiency. Some of its achievements include:

- Building 425 custom reports that include information essential to managers.
- It reduced the number of employees who were working on report management from four to one.
- It eliminated report generation from the nightly update and shortened operations processing by one hour.

- It increased the number of employees who were using the system to access reports by a factor of ten, from the initial 60 to 600.

Source: (https://www.fiserv.com/resources/Business_Analytics_-
_Columbia_State_Bank.pdf)

Case Study #2: MCB Bank

The MCB Bank is one of the largest banks in Pakistan that selected the Oracle's FLEXCUBE Universal Banking system for its international operations. The bank has its offices in three countries (India, UAE, and the United States). The primary goal of the system was to support its centralized operations while serving its customers in an efficient manner.

The previous system could not provide periodic updates on their customer operations. The bank wanted to have an understanding of customer activities to tailor their banking solutions, which promoted their services. Because their system was unintegrated, providing real-time data for analytics was a major challenge.

After a careful evaluation of their operations, the Bank decided to use BI (the bank engaged Techlogix) for the development of a system to achieve efficiency and control in its financial reporting processes.

Working together, Techlogix and MCB Bank successfully implemented the BI system. For this reason, MCB has been able to achieve the following results:

- Launch a comprehensive banking product portfolio that is competitive in the UAE market because they were able to predict their customers' behavior patterns.
- Optimize the operational expenses for the UAE operations by keeping a large portion of the development team offsite.
- Automated complex clearing and fund transfer processes with the BI system.

Source: (http://techlogix.com/wp-content/uploads/2016/04/case-study-MCB-FlexCube.pdf)

Case Study #3: Gulf Insurance Company

Gulf Insurance Company is a large international leading insurance provider based in the Gulf region with over 52 million clients worldwide. The firm was experiencing the following challenges:

- Competition - financial partners were providing similar services and taking away large chunks of customers.
- Economic recessionary trends - significantly reduced their customer base.
- They were unable to understand their customers as other providers were adopting customer-centric approaches.

Because of these challenges, the Gulf Insurance Company almost lost its business. As part of the management strategy, the company decided to roll out an ambitious plan to invest in a BI system that could analyze their customers' behavior with an aim to tailor their products.

Their system was upgraded to BI to provide records from large chunks of unintegrated data. In addition to incidences, transitions, terminations, and utilization, the BI system was programmed to provide reporting and analytics for its Long Term Care product. This included management reporting, fraud detection, and other ad hoc data analysis.

Because of the adoption of the BI system, the Gulf Insurance Company has been able to provide consistent analytics and improve its overall profitability by developing new products that are customer-centric.

Source: (https://www.GulfInsuranceCompany.com/wp-content/uploads/2015/12/Business-Intelligence-implementaton-for-a-Leading-insurance.pdf)

Chapter 9

Future – Smart Contracts and Data Analytics

Even though we have focused on Excel, Python, MatLab, Perl, R, and Java as some of the important tools that are necessary for data analytics, it is important to mention here that technology is changing fast.

Therefore, expect some disruptive technologies to come onboard and destabilize the conventional systems with which you are familiar. If there is one trend that is fueling the rise of these technologies, then it is big data. In the past, firms have used to structure data that could be analyzed and organized into tables easily.

Today, things are different. Organizations are processing massive amounts of data that they have never witnessed before. To make matters more complex, this data is voluminous, semi-structured—in some cases, it is unstructured— and has high velocity. At this rate, the conventional systems may not be sufficient.

That is why smart contracts are being hailed as the future technology.

Smart contracts are computer program codes with the ability to facilitate, execute, and enforce negotiations or performance of an agreement—contract—using the Blockchain technology. These codes can act as substitutes for legal contracts where the contracts are encoded in a computer programming language as a set of instructions.

The potential to link smart contracts to data science is perhaps one of the first steps towards creating a new world of opportunities.

The inclusion of data science capabilities to smart contracts may promote self-enforcing financial contracts—features that execute without a third party. For instance, a farmer can hedge his/her farm produce by using smart contracts which are dependent on various future prices that are based on prevailing data analytics.

If the conditions for the smart contracts are met, the system can automatically send payments to the farmer. This is true for future smart contracts because the farmer will have a physical presence where readily available measures are incorporated into legal systems when the produce is not transferred.

However, smart contracts to enforce data science may immediately find their potential in digital transfer of goods and services where payment and transfer of payments is automatic. At the scale that is dependent on the type of contractual agreement, such automated processes may save billions of dollars and improve the efficiency of their operations.

Nevertheless, the use of smart contracts in these areas is yet to be seen. The enforcement of smart contracts in code form and prevailing laws and regulations in practice still represent a major challenge that has to be resolved in order to realize true potentials of smart contracts in data science.

CONCLUSION

Today, the global economic environment represents a fast-paced and ever changing environment. Today, companies must not only compete in faster ROI but they also face stiff competition. In addition to these challenges, firms have to contend with the demographic changes and developing web 2.0 technologies.

Data analytics provides the only hope for fact-based and insightful-driven decisions to help organizations manage their strategic, operating, and financial performance. In addition, data analytics can help in creating shareholder value. That is why it is no longer tenable to ignore data analytics.

I hope that you have grasped all the basics of data analytics and its role in organizations.

NOTES

These websites can help you explore more about data analytics

1. https://www.sas.com
2. https://halobi.com/2016/07/descriptive-predictive-and-prescriptive-analytics-explained/
3. https://www.dezyre.com/article/types-of-analytics-descriptive-predictive-prescriptive-analytics/209
4. https://www.lynda.com/Hadoop-tutorials/Data-Analysis-Hadoop/460439-2.html
5. http://www.kdnuggets.com/2014/06/top-10-data-analysis-tools-business.html
6. http://www.informationbuilders.com/data-analysis
7. https://ori.hhs.gov/education/products/n_illinois_u/datamanagement/datopic.html
8. http://www.bigskyassociates.com/blog/bid/356764/5-Most-Important-Methods-For-Statistical-Data-Analysis
9. http://www.thearling.com/text/dmwhite/dmwhite.htm
10. http://www.makeuseof.com/tag/create-free-survey-collect-data-excel/
11. https://oit.utk.edu/research/documentation/Documents/HowToUseExcelForDataEntry.pdf
12. https://www.skillsyouneed.com/num/statistics-identifying-patterns.html

13. http://homepages.rpi.edu/~bennek/class/mmld/talks/lecture2-05.ppt

14. https://www.fiserv.com/resources/Business_Analytics_-_Columbia_State_Bank.pdf

15. http://techlogix.com/wp-content/uploads/2016/04/case-study-MCB-FlexCube.pdf

16. https://www.GulfInsuranceCompany.com/wp-content/uploads/2015/12/Business-Intelligence-implementaton-for-a-Leading-insurance.pdf

ABOUT THE AUTHOR

Victor Finch is a zealous enthusiast for the latest technology, innovative gadgets and financial subjects ranging from Fintech to stock trading. These interests strike a deep resonating chord in his passions. He is an entrepreneur, an IT consultant, and a part-time author.

Victor as a child was always fascinated with how things worked; breaking apart his childhood toys is a common sight. Victor always has some innovative workarounds or solutions for his friends or family's problems such as a stubborn laptop that just like to "sleep" and how to improve the quality of life for his family.

If you spot someone, penning down his thoughts while walking down the streets of New York. That could be our dear Victor. He is always intrigued by the latest creativities around and just wants to tinkle with them when he has some me time.

In his spare time, Victor likes to explore the world, read his favorite books, open his little notes and write his next bestseller book.

Victor's Message

Thank you for reading! This book is a starter quick guide on Data Analytics to help you familiarize with the basic understanding on how to read, analyze data with entry level tools in your projects or businesses. Data Analytics is just the tip of the iceberg and there are many more advanced concepts and tools for you to discover on the next book, especially on big data.

If you would like to read more great books like this one, why not subscribe to our website and *follow me here*.

https://www.auvapress.com/vip

Thanks for reading! Please add your short review on Amazon

And let me know what your thoughts! - Victor

Other Victor's Titles You Will Find Useful

Blockchain Technology (#1 Amazon Bestseller)

Blockchain is a revolution that you should not ignore anymore.
Imagine you are been presented with an opportunity before the flourishing of Internet, what would you do? Now is the time!

- You will understand everything you need to know about the mechanics of Blockchain.
- You will learn how you can benefit from Blockchain
- You will learn the legal implications of Blockchain technology

Victor Finch
ISBN: 978-1-5413-6684-8
Paperback: 102 Pages
eBook, Audiobook Available

Bitcoin

Are you still wondering or clueless about what is Bitcoin? Do you know Bitcoin is thriving robustly as a digital currency because of its characteristics for more than 8 years.

You will understand everything (including merits & demerits) you need to know about Bitcoin
You will learn how to use Bitcoin and read the transactions.
You will learn discover the best practices in using Bitcoin securely.

Victor Finch
ISBN: 978-1-5441-4139-8
Paperback: 98 Pages
eBook, Audiobook Available

Other Auva Press Titles You Will Find Useful

Smart Contracts

Smart Contract is about the revolutionary (Blockchain Technology) approach with legal contracts or any legal agreements. This book offers an unprecedented peek into what the future may be like that could possibly change and enhance the traditional way of doing things for the better (many benefits).

- You will learn how disruptive (positive) are Smart Contracts
- You will learn about the legal perspectives of Smart Contracts.
- BONUS Highlight: More than 7 Possible Smart Contract Use Cases in different industries.

Victor Finch
ISBN: 978-1-5446-9150-3
Paperback: 106 Pages
eBook, Audiobook Available

Python

Python is a highly sought after skillset by many corporations. Possibilities with Python are limitless and often prefer over Java and C++ due to three characteristics that you will discover in this book.

- You will learn how to set up your first python.
- You will learn how to properly do error handling and debug to save you hours of time.
- BONUSES Included (plus Hands On Challenges)

Ronald Olsen

ISBN: 978-1-5426-6789-0

Paperback: 152 Pages

eBook, Audiobook Available

AUVA PRESS

AUVA Press commits lots of effort in the content research, planning and production of quality books. Every book is created with you in mind and you will receive the best possible valuable information in clarity and accomplish your goals.

If you like what you have seen and benefited from this helpful book, we would appreciate your honest review on Amazon or on your favorite social media.

Your review is appreciated and will go a long way to motivate us in producing more quality books for your reading pleasure and needs.

Visit Us Online

AUVA PRESS Books
https://www.auvapress.com/books

Register for Updates
https://www.auvapress.com/vip

Contact Us

AUVA Press books may be purchased in bulk for corporate, academic, gifts or promotional use.

For information on translation, licenses, media requests, please visit our contact page.
https://www.auvapress.com/contact

- END -